Back to Basics

ENGLISH

for 7-8 year olds

Sheila Lane and Marion Kemp

Letts

The alphabet

The capital letters are: A B C D E F G H I J K L M N O P Q R S T U V W X Y Z
The small letters are: a b c d e f g h i j k l m n o p q r s t u v w x y z

Fill in the missing capital and small letters.

A			D			G			J			M	N					S			V	W			Z
	b	c		e	f		h	i		k	l			o	p	q	r		t	u			x	y	

Write the letters again in the empty rings. Put them in **alphabetical order**. The first one is done for you to show you what to do.

1	m	k	n	l	k	l	m	n
2	v	x	w	u				
3	r	o	q	p				
4	h	f	i	g				
5	e	d	b	c				

Write each set of words in **alphabetical order**.
The first one is done for you.

1	bear	dog	ant	ant	bear	dog
2	leg	arm	toe			
3	hat	coat	shoe			
4	Tom	Carol	Janet			
5	zoo	sty	den			
6	cat	pig	dog			

Sets

Finish each sentence:

Janet's book is about ______________________________

Tom is reading about ______________________________

Read the names of these **sets** of things.

fruits	vegetables	trees
colours	clothes	insects

Here are 3 sets of pictures:

Fill in the name of each set.

1  These are all trees.

2  These are all ______________

3  These are all ______________

Here are 3 more sets:

Write a sentence for each set.

1  These are all colours.

2  ______________________________

3  ______________________________

Here are 3 more sets:

Add more names to each one.

TOYS 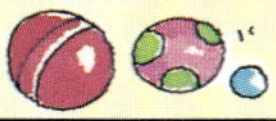	**BIRDS** 	**ANIMALS** 
ball	robin	cat

Sentences

A **sentence** begins with a capital letter and ends with a full stop.

Can you read this sentence?

Jackandhismotherwerepoor.

Pull the words apart like this:

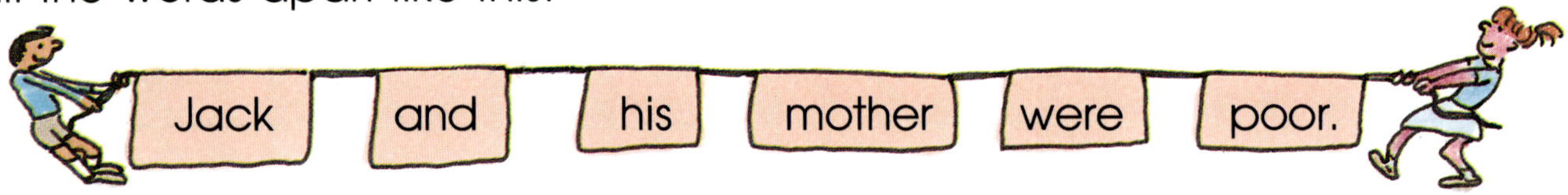

Now read the sentence. Jack and his mother were poor.

Write these sentences with a space between each word:

1 Jacktooktheirlittlecowtomarket.

2 Hesoldthecowforfivebeans.

3 Jack'smotherwasveryangry.

4 Shethrewthebeansoutofthewindow.

Write the 4 sentences correctly.

the puppet ran away from his master once there was a wicked witch the king rode a beautiful white horse by morning the straw was spun into gold

Spelling

Write the missing letters in the alphabet.

a _ _ _ e _ _ _ i _ _ _ _ _ o _ _ _ _ _ u _ _ _ _ _

Check your alphabet from page 2.

The letters **a e i o u** are called **vowels**.

The letters you have written in are called **consonants**.

Make words by putting in **vowels**.
Choose a different vowel for each set.

1	2	3	4	5	6
b _ g	p _ t	d _ g	t _ p	f _ n	h _ t
b _ g	p _ t	d _ g	t _ p	f _ n	h _ t
b _ g	p _ t	d _ g	t _ p	f _ n	h _ t

Sometimes the letter **y** is used as a vowel.

Write the letter **y** to complete each word.

b _   c r _   m _   t r _   f l _   s t _   d r _   w h _

Use the words you have made to complete these sentences:

1 The _ _ _ flew _ _.

2 Don't give up, just _ _ _.

3 The opposite of wet is _ _ _.

4 Where's _ _ coat?

5 The pigs were in a _ _ _.

6 _ _ _ did Pat _ _ _ ?

Understanding a story

The story of The Lion and the Mouse has been written without capital letters or full stops.
Can you read it in one breath?

> a mighty lion caught a tiny mouse in its paw the lion agreed to let the little mouse go free some time later the lion was trapped in a net the mouse gnawed away the ropes and set the lion free

Write the story in 4 sentences.

Write the missing words from the story.

1 The lion caught a mouse in its ______ .

2 The lion let the little mouse _____ ________ .

3 Later the lion was ____________ in a ______ .

4 The __________ gnawed away at the __________ and the _________ was set free.

Which is it?

Write the missing vowels in the alphabet.

_	b	c	d	_	f	g	h	_	j	k	l	m	n	_	p	q	r	s	t	_	v	w	x	y	z

Do you write **an** or **a**?

Always write **an** before words beginning with vowels.	Always write **a** before words beginning with consonants.

Fill in each space with **an** or **a**.

_____ egg _____ hat _____ tree _____ umbrella _____ ball

_____ owl _____ arm _____ island _____ flower _____ man

_______ old hat _______ pretty picture _______ angry face

_______ new coat _______ ugly duckling _______ happy teacher

Do you write **to** or **two**?

to

I went **to** the Zoo.

two

I have **two** ears.

Fill in each space with **to** or **two**.

1 Ten and _________ make twelve.

2 Ahmet went _________ see Neil and Mary.

3 I walk _________ school with my friends.

4 At _________ o'clock I am going out _________ meet Karen.

5 My _______ best friends are coming _________ tea on Sunday.

Sentences

Read this muddled sentence: went to the park children The

Read this sensible sentence: The children went to the park.

Write each group of words in the right order to make a sensible sentence. Remember the full stop.

1 were playing rounders Diana and her friends

___

2 playing football enjoys Robert

___

3 Lucy to see her grandmother went

___

4 and whales swim Sharks water in

___

5 aeroplanes fly Birds in the air and

___

6 in trees Most apes and live monkeys

___

Puzzle corner

How many different sentences can you make from the **sentence machine**?

The alphabet

Fill in all the missing capital and small letters.

A _ _ _ _ _ _ H _ _ _ _ _ _ _ O _ _ _ _ _ _ _ _ _ _ _ Z

a _ _ _ _ _ _ _ _ _ k _ _ _ _ _ _ _ _ _ _ _ _ _ _ z

Check your alphabet from page 2.

Fill in the answers to these questions about the 26 letters of the alphabet:

1 The last letter of the alphabet is ______.
2 The fifth letter of the alphabet is ______.
3 The letter before w is ______.
4 The letter before m is ______.
5 The letters on each side of g are ______ and ______ .

These letters are in alphabetical order, but some have been left out.

Write the word which the missing letters spell.

1	k l _ n _ _ q	m o p
2	e _ g h _ j k l m _	_ _ _
3	r _ _ u v w x _ z	_ _ _
4	a _ c d _ f _ h	_ _ _
5	_ _ p q r s _ u	_ _ _

Add **one** straight line to make each shape into a capital letter like this:

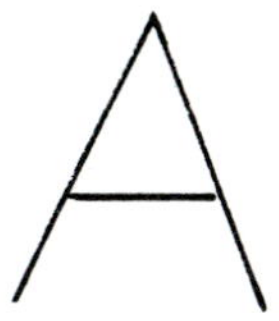

Spelling

Say the sound of each of these consonants: b n d j p g c t m s

Write the first letter of each word to make a new word.

1 pencil ink gate

___ ___ ___ = ______

2 ball elephant dog

___ ___ ___ = ______

3 mouse apple needle

___ ___ ___ = ______

4 cup orange tree

___ ___ ___ = ______

5 window elephant tree

___ ___ ___ = ______

6 snake umbrella needle

___ ___ ___ = ______

Say the sound of this consonant: **s**
Say the sound of this consonant: **h**

Push the **two** sounds together to make **one** sound like this: s h   s h

s p   s t   s w

Complete each word with **sh**, **sp**, **st** or **sw**.

1 _ _ ider   2 _ _ ip   3 _ _ ick   4 _ _ im

5 fi _ _   6 wa _ _   7 bru _ _   8 ne _ _

Complete each sentence with the right word.

1 I can ________ well. (shell / spell)

2 I like to eat ________ . (sweets / sheets)

3 ________ swim in the sea. (Sparks / Sharks)

4 Monkeys ________ in the trees. (sting / swing)

Sets

Fill in the blank card to make a **set** of things you can **eat**.

Here are 4 more sets:

Add more names to each one.

Drinks	Clothes	Homes	Shapes
lemonade	trousers	bungalow	circle

Draw a (ring) round the word which does **not** belong to the set.

1 table bed stool (house) chair

2 three four six nine triangle

3 Sunday week Thursday Monday Friday

4 John Ann girl Pat Alan

5 sugar butter cheese salt plate

Write the name of the book which does **not** belong to the set on the shelf.

____

Sentences

Colour in the big question mark.

Here are some **question** words:

Which? Where? How? Who? What? When? Why?

Match each **question** with the right answer from the bunch of balloons. Write the answers on the lines.

1 Which day comes after Sunday?

____

2 Which is more... 3+3 or 3+2?

____

3 When is Christmas Day?

____

4 How many letters are there in the alphabet?

____

5 What do you call your mother's brother?

____

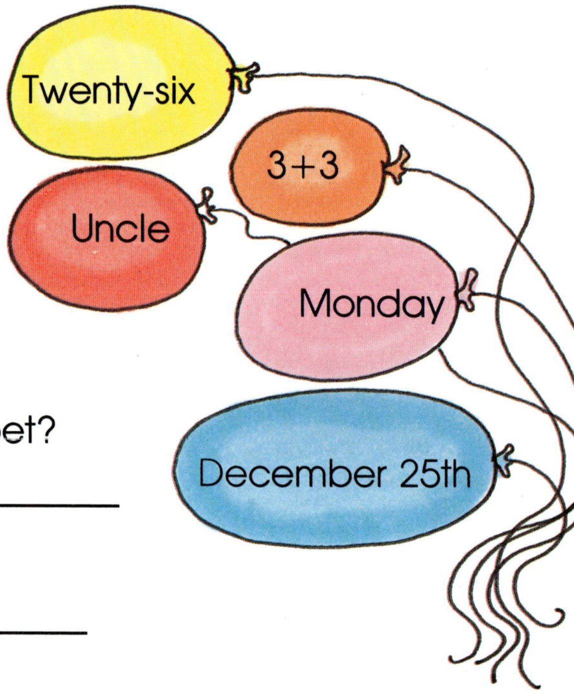

Match each answer with the right **question** from the balloons. Write the **questions** on the lines.

1 ______________________________

A watch dog

2 ______________________________

A horse.

3 ______________________________

When you are a mouse.

Which book?

Read these questions:

Which book would give you the answers? Write the **title** of the book each time.

1 Can all birds fly? ______________________

2 Which fish live in rivers? ______________________

3 Which farm animals lay eggs? ______________________

4 Do fish lay eggs? ______________________

5 What colour are robins' eggs? ______________________

Read the **contents** page of a book about farm animals.

Write the number of the page where you could find out about:

CONTENTS	*page*
Hens and chickens	4
Animals which give milk	9
Caring for pigs	14
Sheep	20
Farm horses	26

1 Chickens . . . page ____

2 Lambs . . . page ____

3 Piglets . . . page ____

4 Calves . . . page ____

5 Foals . . . page ____

Puzzle corner

Write the names of the baby animals correctly.

____

____

____

Naming words

Read this list of **naming words**:

Tick the names of things which you can wear.

ball	doll	sandal
slipper	poppy	shoe
rose	jigsaw	lily

Write the names from the box under the correct shop.

TOY SHOP 

FLOWER SHOP 

SHOE SHOP 

Naming words are called **nouns**.

Read this list of **nouns**:

chimney	stairs	walls	tyres	horn	wheel
window	brake	door	wiper	gutter	knocker

Write the **nouns** in the correct shape.

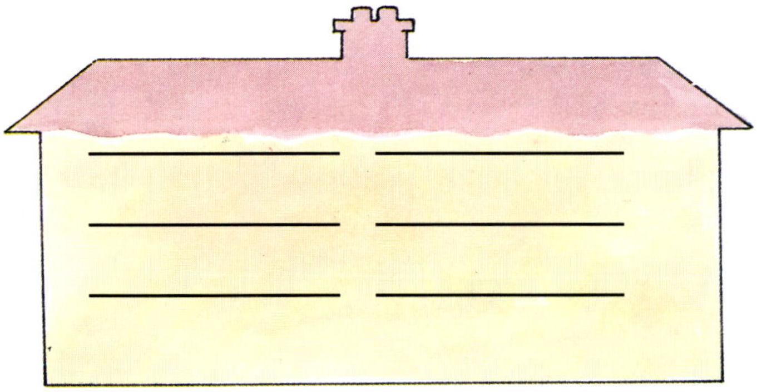

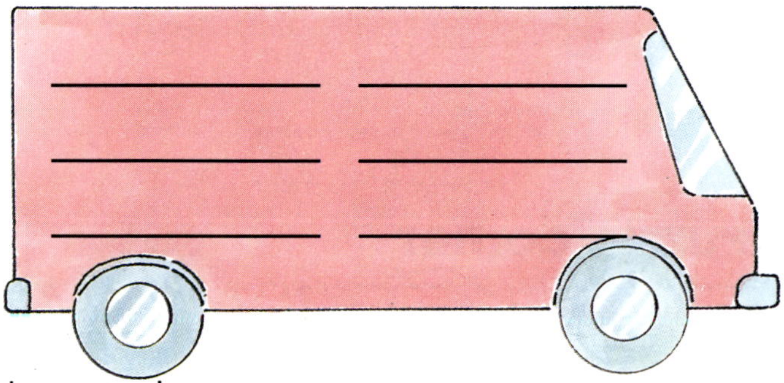

Write each **noun** as a separate word.

appleinkeelowlumbrella

Sentences

What is in the Christmas stocking? Write here:

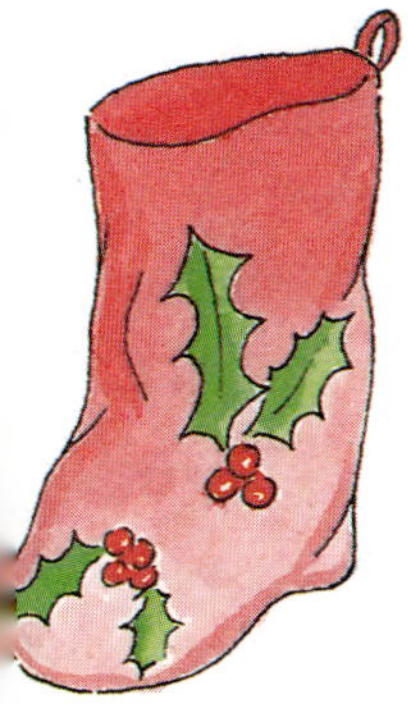

a juicy
of slippers
a pack
a book
of cards

of sweets
a pair
orange
a box
of puzzles

1 a juicy orange
2 ______
3 ______
4 ______
5 ______

Match the two parts of each sentence.

1 On Christmas Day — shines with fairy lights.
2 I can't wait — I wake up early.
3 Our Christmas tree — to our friends.
4 We eat — roast turkey for dinner.
5 We sing carols — to open my presents.

Write the complete sentences here:

1 ______
2 ______
3 ______
4 ______
5 ______

Write the mixed-up words in the right order to make a sensible sentence.

1 The is name in of the Puss pantomime Boots.

______

2 The Beanstalk of name and Jack is the pantomime the.

______

______

What's the same?

Write a sentence to answer each question.

1 What's the same about a hat and a cap?

____

2 What's the same about shoes and slippers?

____

Some words mean the **same** or almost the same as other words.

a <u>little</u> ant   a <u>tiny</u> ant

a <u>small</u> ant

Join the words which have the **same** meaning.

big	tiny	end	ill
start	large	sick	stop
small	begin	halt	finish

Complete each sentence.

1 Small means the same as ______________ .

2 Another word for finish is ______________ .

3 Someone who is ill is ______________ .

4 Another word for large is ______________ .

5 To start is to ______________ .

6 To halt is to ______________ .

What's different?

Some words mean the **opposite** of other words.

Join the words which have the **opposite** meanings.

push	cold	low	sweet
hot	long	happy	high
tiny	pull	sour	dirty
short	quick	clean	sad
slow	huge	shut	ugly
good	bad	pretty	open

Write the **opposite** of the word in the bracket in the space.

1 a ____________ face (sad)

2 a ____________ apple (good)

3 an ____________ door (shut)

4 a ____________ plate (clean)

5 a ____________ orange (sour)

6 a ____________ train (quick)

Complete each sentence with an **opposite**.

1 Fire is hot, but ice is ____________ .

2 A mouse is ____________ , but an elephant is ____________ .

3 A rabbit has a short neck, but a giraffe's neck is ____________ .

4 A bungalow is a low building, but a tower is ____________ .

5 A sheep is a tame animal, but a lion is ____________ .

Which is it?

Do you write **is** or **are**?

is

This **is** a girl.

are

These **are** the children.

Always write **is** for **one** person or thing.
Always write **are** for **more than one**.

Complete each sentence with **is** or **are**.

1 A robin ______ a bird. **2** Robins ______ birds.

3 A bee ______ an insect. **4** Bees ______ insects.

5 A tadpole ______ a young frog. **6** Lambs ______ young sheep.

7 A baby horse ______ called a foal. **8** Kittens ______ baby cats.

9 A cygnet ______ a young swan. **10** Puppies ______ young dogs.

Do you write **is** or **his**?

his means: belonging to him

is

This **is** Tom's ball.

his

Tom kicked **his** ball.

Complete each sentence with **is** or **his**.

1 Paul made a card for ______ sister.

2 Jane ______ coming to play today.

3 Susan ______ wearing her new coat.

4 Peter ______ eight years old, but ______ brother ______ only three.

5 Ben's aunt came to tea, but ______ uncle did not come because he ______ at work.

Spelling

Some **double words** are made by joining two shorter words together like this:

Join these short words together to make **double words**.

some	get	bath	fish
out	stairs	water	day
can	side	gold	fall
down	not	birth	board
for	thing	cup	room

Complete these word sums to make **double words**.

1 snow + ________ = snowball

2 tea + ________ = teaspoon

3 ________ + hat = sunhat

4 book + shelf = ________

5 farm + ________ = farmhouse

6 ________ + bow = rainbow

7 arm + chair = ________

8 life + ________ = lifeboat

9 ________ + noon = afternoon

10 news + paper = ________

Write the **same** missing word under each picture to make a **double word**.

fire ________

police ________

snow ________

milk ________

Action words

Answer the questions by reading the chart.

	swim	fly	walk
cod	✓	✗	✗
dog	✓	✗	✓
owl	✗	✓	✓

1 What can walk and swim but not fly?

2 What can fly and walk but not swim?

Draw a ring round the **action** word in each sentence.

1 Harry lost his coat.

2 Alan ate an orange.

3 Bob undid the knot.

4 Liam gave a present.

5 Jean heard the music.

Write the **action** word in the puzzle.

1 l	o	s	t	
2				
3				
4				
5				

An **action** word is called a **verb**.

Write the **verb** going down from 1-5.

_ _ _ _ _

Read this story:

Once there was a class of very noisy children. They laughed and shouted. They thumped and bumped. They even banged and whistled.

Draw a ring round the things which the children did to make a noise. These are called **verbs**.

Write the **verbs** here: ______ ______

______ ______ ______ ______

Sentences

Read these sentences:

Everyone enjoyed eating it.

Mrs Cook made a cake.

She put it in the oven to bake.

Write the sentences under the pictures in the right order.

Write each set of sentences in the right order.

He got on the bus.	______________________
He got off the bus.	______________________
Tom went to the bus stop.	______________________
Kim stuck a pin in it.	______________________
Pat blew up a balloon.	______________________
The balloon burst.	______________________
She fell to the ground.	______________________
Janvir climbed up a tree.	______________________
The branch snapped.	______________________

Right order

The days of the week are:

Friday Tuesday
Monday Thursday Wednesday
Sunday Saturday

Write the days of the week in the **right order**.

Start with Sunday.

1 ____________ first
2 ____________ second
3 ____________ third
4 ____________ fourth
5 ____________ fifth
6 ____________ sixth
7 ____________ seventh

Complete these sentences:

1 Monday is the __second__ day of the week.
2 The ____________ day is Saturday.
3 Thursday is the ____________ day.
4 The name of the ____________ day is Tuesday.
5 Wednesday is the ____________ day.

Write the number words in order of size starting with the smallest.

1	eight	six	two
	__two__	____________	____________
2	four	twelve	ten
	____________	____________	____________
3	sixteen	twelve	fifteen
	____________	____________	____________
4	thirteen	nine	three
	____________	____________	____________

Is it true?

Which is the true sentence?

Scissors cut.

or

Scissors sing.

The true sentence is: Scissors cut.

Write the **true** sentence.

1 Fish swim in the sea.
Fish swim on land. ______________________________

2 We go to bed to sleep.
We go to bed to fly. ______________________________

3 The cook boiled an egg.
The cook laid an egg. ______________________________

4 Snails move quickly.
Snails move slowly. ______________________________

Draw a ring round the **right word** for each sentence.

1 Dogs have four tails. / ears. / legs.

2 I can see through glass. / wood. / bricks.

3 A car runs on water. / milk. / petrol.

4 Houses have doors. / horns. / wheels.

5 We hear with our feet. / eyes. / ears.

6 Dentists care for our toes. / teeth. / fingers.

Information

The African elephant is the largest land animal. It can weigh 6 tonnes.

The giraffe is the tallest animal. It can grow to a height of 6 metres.

The cheetah is the fastest runner. It can move at 112 kilometres an hour.

The humming bird is the smallest bird. It can fit inside an egg-cup.

Write the answers in the box.

1 Which animal is the tallest?

2 What is the name of the smallest bird?

3 What can an African elephant weigh?

4 How fast can a cheetah run?

Choose the correct word from the brackets and write the complete sentence.

1 The largest (sea, land) animal is the African elephant.

2 The (shortest, tallest) of the animals is the giraffe.

3 The humming bird can fit inside an (egg-cup, teapot).

4 The fastest (swimmer, runner) of all the animals is a cheetah.

Same and different

Look at the words round the sun.
Some of them mean the **same** as **bright**.

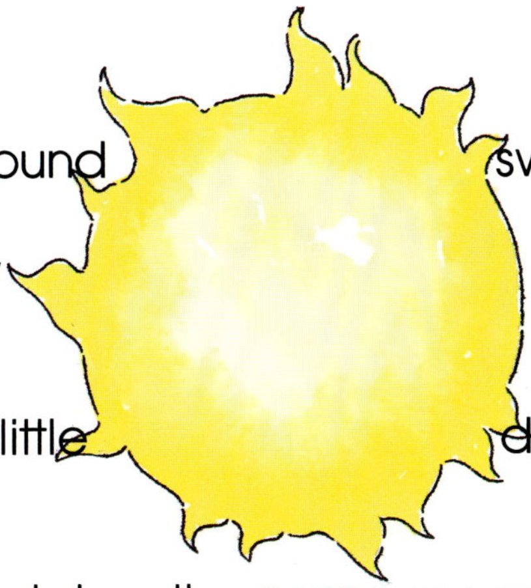

Write the words which mean **bright** inside the sun.

Draw a (ring) round the word which has the **same** meaning as the one in the box.

1	small	smell	little	mouse	ant
2	begin	end	bend	start	run
3	plump	pig	lump	thin	fat
4	fast	quick	last	key	door
5	talk	stalk	speak	sleep	walk

Write the words which mean the **opposite** of **hot** inside the snowman.

Draw a (ring) round the word which has the **opposite** meaning to the one in the box.

1	bad	bud	good	dog	bed
2	dry	try	laugh	cry	wet
3	old	new	you	gold	cold
4	clean	white	nice	dirty	brown
5	wrong	cross	right	sum	word

Thinking about nouns

A **name** is the word by which something is known.	All words which are **names** are called **nouns**.	Ordinary names are called **common nouns**.

Read all the words in the box.

Draw a (ring) round each word which is a **common noun**.

pencil	chair	open	eat	spade
write	sit	door	cake	dig

Write the 5 **common nouns** here:

__________ __________ __________ __________ __________

Write one of the 5 **common nouns** in each sentence.

1 I can sit on a __________ .

2 A gardener can dig with a __________ .

3 My dog can open the __________ with his paw.

4 I like a sharp __________ when I write.

5 I could eat a big, cream __________ .

What can you eat?

Pull the **nouns** apart.

Write the 5 **common nouns**.

Thinking about verbs

Action words tell us what is **being done** in a sentence.

Action words are called **verbs**.

Read all the words in the box.

Draw a (ring) round each word which is a **verb**.

pencil	chair	open	eat	spade
write	sit	door	cake	dig

Write the 5 **verbs** here:

__________ __________ __________ __________ __________

Write <u>one</u> of the **verbs** in each sentence.

1 I can __________ on a chair.

2 A gardener can __________ with a spade.

3 My dog can __________ the door with his paw.

4 I like a sharp pencil when I __________ .

5 I could __________ a big, cream cake.

What can you do?

Pull the **verbs** apart.

Write the 5 **verbs**.

Spelling

Two sounds can be pushed together to make **one** sound like this:

c h | w h | t h

Write **two** letters which sound together to complete each word.

		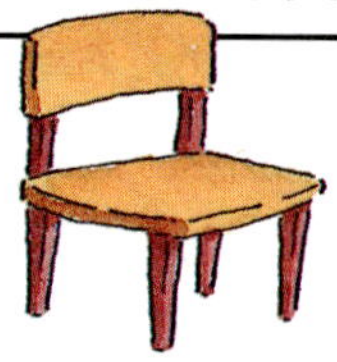	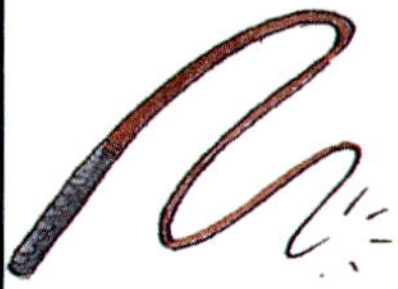		
_ _ ree	_ _ eel	_ _ air	_ _ ip	_ _ erry	_ _ irty

Here are more sounds which can be pushed together:

dr bl fl cl cr fr

Write **two** letters which sound together to complete each word.

_ _ og	_ _ ock	_ _ own	_ _ um	_ _ ue	_ _ ag

Write the answer in the sentence and in the puzzle, using the words you have made.

1 ________ is the name of a colour.

2 A ________ tells the time.

3 A king wears a ________ .

4 A ________ can be used to give a signal.

5 You can beat a ________ .

6 A tadpole is a young ________ .

1 b	l	u	e	
2				
3				
4				
5				
6				

True or not true

Study each of these flags.

Great Britain

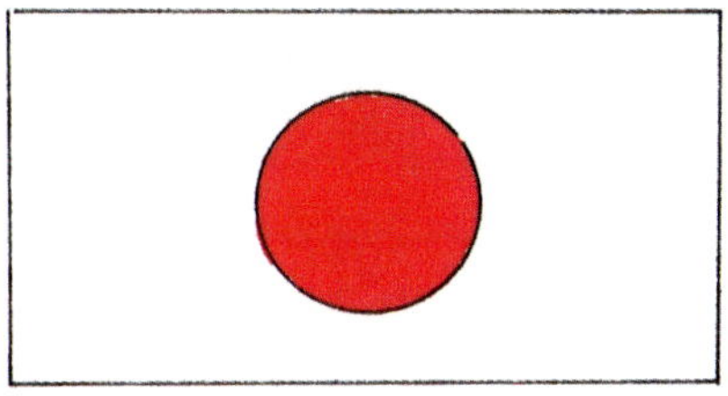
Japan

Canada

Denmark

Turkey

India

Write `true` or `not true` at the end of each sentence.

1 Japan's flag is a red circle on a white background.

2 The leaf on Canada's flag is coloured green.

3 The flag of Denmark is a white cross on a red background.

4 All six flags are coloured in red and white.

5 Turkey's flag has a yellow moon and a yellow star.

6 In the middle of India's flag there is a small wheel.

7 Britain's flag is a white cross on a red background.

8 The flag of the Olympic Games has five rings.

Rhymes

Words which have the same sounds at the ends are called **rhymes**.

Make **pairs of rhymes** from the words in the box like this:

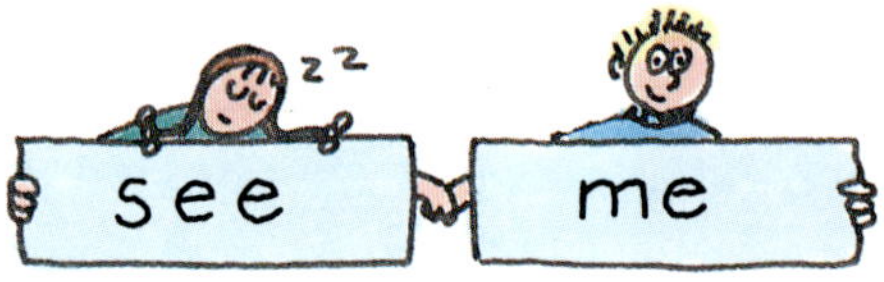

leg	ship	back
see	coat	sing
wing	trip	boat
wag	sack	bag
me	beg	

In each line write 4 more words which **rhyme** with the word in the box like this: Jan   c a n   m a n   r a n   p a n

bat	c _ _	f _ _	s _ _	p _ _
get	w _ _	l _ _	m _ _	s _ _
pin	b _ _	w _ _	t _ _	f _ _
hot	p _ _	c _ _	r _ _	l _ _
mug	b _ _	r _ _	h _ _	t _ _

Finish each of the following with a rhyming word:

1 Hark! Hark!
The dogs do ____________ .

2 Rain, Rain! Go away,
Come again another ____________ .

3 Twinkle, twinkle little ________
How I wonder what you are!

4 Riddle me! Riddle me! What is that:
Over your head and under your
____________ ?

Memorizing

Say the names of the 12 things in the picture.
When you are ready, cover the picture.

Draw or write all the things you can remember in each set.

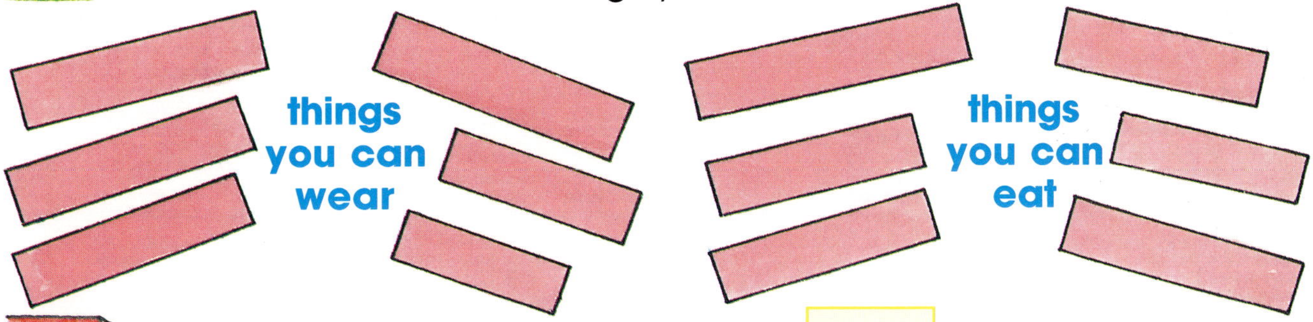

Write how many you remembered.

There are 6 sets of rhymes in the picture.
When you are ready, cover the picture.

Write all the things you can remember in rhyme sets.

sun
gun
bun

Write how many you remembered.

Answers

Answers to alphabet questions on pp 2, 5, 7 and 9 can be checked from the alphabet on p2.

P2

2 arm	leg	toe
3 coat	hat	shoe
4 Carol	Janet	Tom
5 den	sty	zoo
6 cat	dog	pig

P3

2 fruits
3 vegetables

2 These are all clothes.
3 These are all insects.

P4

The puppet...
Once there...
The King...
By morning...

P5

1 a,e,i,o *or* u   2 a,e,i,o *or* u
3 i,o *or* u   4 a,i *or* o
5 a,e,i *or* u   6 a,e,i,o *or* u

by cry my try fly sty dry why

1 fly, by   2 try
3 dry   4 my
5 sty   6 why, cry

P6

A mighty lion...
The lion agreed...
Some time later...
The mouse...

1 paw
2 go free
3 trapped, net
4 mouse, ropes, lion

P7

an egg **a** hat **a** tree
an umbrella
a ball **an** owl **an** arm
an island **a** flower
a man

an old hat **a** pretty picture
an angry face **a** new coat
an ugly duckling **a** happy teacher

1 two   4 two, to
2 to   5 two, to
3 to

P8

1 Diana and her friends were playing rounders.
2 Robert enjoys playing football.
3 Lucy went to see her grandmother.
4 Sharks and whales swim in water.
5 Birds and aeroplanes fly in the air.
6 Most apes and monkeys live in trees.

P9

2 fin   4 beg
3 sty   5 not

P10

2 beg   5 wet
3 man   6 sun
4 cot

1 **sp**ider   5 fi**sh**/**st**
2 **sh**ip   6 wa**sp**/**sh**
3 **st**ick   7 **br**ush
4 **sw**im   8 ne**st**

1 spell   3 Sharks
2 sweets   4 swing

P11

2 triangle
3 week
4 girl
5 plate

Dictionary

P12

1 Monday
2 3 + 3
3 December 25th
4 twenty-six
5 Uncle

1 Which dog keeps the best time?
2 Which animal goes to bed with its shoes on?
3 When is it bad luck to be followed by a black cat?

P13

1 Birds of the Air
2 Fish of the Sea
3 Farm Animals
4 Fish of the Sea
5 Birds of the Air

1 4   4 9
2 20   5 26
3 14

puppy kitten duckling

P14

slipper	sandal	shoe
ball	rose	slipper
doll	poppy	sandal
jigsaw	lily	shoe

chimney	brake
window	door
stairs	wiper
knocker	tyres
walls	horn
gutter	wheel

apple ink eel owl umbrella

P15

2 a pack of sweets
3 a book of puzzles
4 a pair of slippers
5 a box of cards

1 ...I wake up early.
2 ...to open my presents.
3 ...shines with fairy lights.
4 ...roast turkey for dinner.
5 ...to our friends.

1 Puss in Boots is the name of the pantomime.
2 Jack in the Beanstalk is the name of the pantomime.

P16

1 You wear them both on your head.
2 You wear them both on your feet.

start	begin
small	tiny
end	finish
sick	ill
halt	stop

1 tiny   4 big
2 end   5 begin
3 sick   6 stop

P17

hot	cold	low	high
tiny	huge	happy	sad
short	long	sour	sweet
slow	quick	clean	dirty
good	bad	shut	open
		pretty	ugly

1 happy   4 dirty
2 bad   5 sweet
3 open   6 slow

1 cold   4 high
2 small, big   5 wild
3 long

P18

1, 3, 5, 7, 9: is
2, 4, 6, 8, 10: are

1 his   4 is, his, is
2 is   5 his, is
3 is

P19

outside	bathroom
cannot	waterfall
downstairs	goldfish
forget	birthday
	cupboard

1 ball   6 rain
2 spoon   7 armchair
3 sun   8 boat
4 bookshelf   9 after
5 mouse   10 newspaper

fire**man**   snow**man**
police**man**   milk**man**

P20

1 dog   2 owl

2 ate
3 undid
4 gave
5 heard

laugh

laughed, shouted, thumped, bumped, banged, whistled

P21

Mrs Cook...
She put...
Everyone...

Tom went...
He got on...
He got off...

Pat blew...
Kim stuck...
The balloon...

Janvir...
The branch...
She fell...

P22

2 seventh   4 third
3 fifth   5 fourth

1 two, six, eight
2 four, ten, twelve
3 twelve, fifteen, sixteen
4 three, nine, thirteen

P23

1 Fish swim in the sea.
2 We go to bed to sleep.
3 The cook boiled an egg.
4 Snails move slowly.

1 legs   2 glass
3 petrol   4 doors
5 ears   6 teeth

P24

1 giraffe   3 6 tonnes
2 humming bird   4 112 kilometres an hour

1 land   3 egg-cup
2 tallest   4 runner

P25

sparkling, dazzling, shiny

1 little   4 quick
2 start   5 speak
3 fat

icy, frosty, cold

1 good   4 dirty
2 wet   5 right
3 new

P26

pencil, chair, spade, door, cake

1 chair   4 pencil
2 spade   5 cake
3 door

egg, jam, bun, pie, chips

P27

open, eat, write, sit, dig

1 sit   4 write
2 dig   5 eat
3 open

run, walk, skip, hop, swim

P28

th, wh, ch, wh, ch, th

fr, cl, cr, dr, bl, fl

2 clock   5 drum
3 crown   6 frog
4 flag

P29

1 true   5 not true
2 not true   6 true
3 true   7 not true
4 not true   8 true

P30

leg, beg   ship, trip
wing, sing   coat, boat
wag, bag   sack, back

cat, fat, sat, pat
wet, let, met, set
bin, win, tin, fin
pot, cot, rot, lot

bug, rug, mug, tug

1 bark   2 day
3 star   4 hat

P31

coat	cap	tart	apple
dress	shirt	fish	milk
sock	shoe	egg	ice-cream

hen	dock	hat	tree	rake
ten, 10	sock	mat	three, 3	cake
pen	lock	cat	bee	snake